The Water Fountain is Empty

K. ROSS

AOS Publishing, 2024

ISBN: 978-1-990496-85-1

Cover Design: Jessica James

Visit AOS Publishing's website:
www.aospublishing.com

Foreword

I began writing this book with the hope of getting my poetry out there. As I started working on it, the words came together to pages and then a book, I realized it had become a synthesis of my life.

Hopefully these pages can inspire someone else to speak their truth.

To the years I spent thinking I was broken. And to all the people looking for reasons to live, the answer is within you.

Dedicated to those who felt everything and nothing all at the same time.

Sound waves

"*No one will love you more than I do*"
Those words,
Uttered by your raspy
Yet sweet voice
Haunt me.
The way those sound waves hit me
Would never compare
To the way those
Words cut deeper.
As if salt seeped
Into my already open wounds.
Moving forward,
With every breath I take
Reminiscing on
The last day
I ever heard,
That raspy,
Yet sweet voice.

Miss me
Miss you
It was always us two

Tumbling

How tragic it is
to witness
Like Jenga blocks,
Brick by brick.
Your vision
Collapsing.
Watching it be taken apart,
So structured, yet so chaotic
Holding your breath.
Anticipating the end.
Still.
You sit and watch
As something you once knew as whole
Comes tumbling down.
Yet when it falls,
You are surprised.
Although you watched it be taken apart,
Knowing it couldn't withstand the lack of support,
You still are in disbelief that it fell apart.

Alternate

As I sit,
I reflect
On how many alternate realities
Could have taken over my life
The present is a tricky thing
One moment can change your life

In one reality
I drink a lukewarm beverage
Constantly.
Straight.
Numbing my pain
A flood of warmth
Washing over my body
As the bitter taste covers my lips
I feel nothing
My eyes slightly close

In another,
I try to focus
My vision is blurred
Loud music surrounds my ears—
The buzzing noise
I feel my blood
It is pulsing through my veins
Something I am no stranger to
My eyes slightly close
I inhale
Then exhale
A thick cloud of smoke engulfs the air

I could also be fine
Nine to five
Rent is due tomorrow
A dirty apron
The smell of fried food
I do what I need to get by
Monday, Tuesday, Wednesday
All days are the same
A continual existence where
I
Do what I need to get by
Fatigue washing over me,
I close my eyes slightly

I reflect
On many alternates to my life
However,
There is one reality
I never dare to consider
It is the one
Where you
                    Are still alive

Flash

I can't remember much
The age of ten to sixteen.
A blur

Almost as though I was on autopilot.
Streaming through the clouds
Drifting by,
Days passing one by one
Until they all added up to my life.
A gentle breeze
Shifting me forward
The comfort of laughter
The numbness of melancholy
Just dull
Flashes of moments
Blinded
By time.

Flushed

I wanted to believe that
I was loved
Cherished
So much so that I created what I believe now to be a false reality
I was dutiful
Polite
Never showing a lack of gratitude
As if you had given me something
When in reality,
Kindness
Shouldn't be considered a reward.
I always considered myself one of you
Did as I was told
Did more than I was asked
I was the ideal
Until I didn't do as you wanted
Kept a secret that was not mine to tell
You threw me aside
Banished me
Threw away the garbage you thought of as an ideal
Because the truth is,
There was no love lost
Because I
Was not the one you shared blood with
People don't like to believe it,
But
Blood and loyalty
Go hand in hand
And even though for years I proved loyalty
Water
When there is no drought
Is no necessity
Water is just something to be ran and flushed down the drain

Stay

Childhood is filled with hope
And the bliss of naïveté
Anything can happen
The future is endless
Childhood is like a wishing fountain
You throw in your penny
And wait for your dreams to come true
I can hear the splash in the water
I can feel the pressure of my eyes shutting
The mini goosebumps
Waiting and waiting
For
My utmost desire.
For you to stay
And never worry
About you going away
And knowing that
We will always stay
Together.

K. Ross

Anchor

I used to anchor you to the sea floor
and you branded that
as my type of love.
So I'll continue to wander at sea,
fearing that I'll drag you down once more.

Ten Thousand Hours

And I wasn't crying because I loved you,
I was crying because
someday I won't anymore.
Incredible how things slip
through your fingers,
and you're forced to
remember the stupid things you've done.
They say it takes
ten thousand hours to master something.
We had four times that
and yet we still fell apart.

Tethered

You and I
Tethered,
A ship sunken
Beneath us
Waves hitting the shore
How many days have passed?
How many words have we left unsaid?
Like the seaside
Sheets soaked
The taste of salt
The only memory that persists
All I can recall
But as the sun rises
The storm stops
And just like that
Another day is upon us
Tethered,
You and I

Name

Your name was
In my mouth like air;
A silent,
Secret burden.
A type of happiness,
Yet slight despair.
Constantly in the depths of my brain
An unconscious,
Yet prevalent thought.
Like a bright summer day overtaken by rain.

Who am I without you?

My admiration for you
Runs deep.
It is as if within my very veins
Is not blood
But rather the being that is you,
As if I could survive
Simply from your glance.
Your words nourish me
And if you, my dear,
Called me
Late one night
And told me
That I
Was the only one you could ever be with
I would rush to your side.
To have if only
One more hour
Wrapped within your
Existence
To have experience
Half your gaze,
I would.
Because
Who am I
Without
Your endless love?

How many?

How many?
How many people in this world have the power to shatter you,
Bring you to your knees,
Make you quiver
And beg for them?
You—
Were you my heartbreak?
A thousand thoughts
Through my mind
For as many times as you called me yours
As many times as you held my heart.
You just sat there,
Eye to eye
Still and quiet
Clenching your fist
As you crushed
The only thing
Keeping me alive.

Impossible endearment

I feel as though
I am pursuing a ghost.
The type of endearment
I long.
I crave.
I seek.
Desire for
A love I have already experienced.
One that is warm
One that is kind
One that is understanding.
As if they are remnants
I can see
But cannot grasp—
Slipping through my fingers
Subtle
A transparent memory
A love that
Takes
An eternity
Unceasing.
The phantom of this love
Keeps me up at night
Wondering,
If I will ever have
Those countless goosebumps
That covered my skin
Or the passion that
Had once
Filled my soul.

Alive

What a true blessing to be able to say that you have found a
love that cuts deep.
One that courses through your veins, nourishing your soul.
What an inspiration to have someone
see you as the only person they could ever love.
What an invitation to allow someone to enter your mind and
witness your soul.
How is there a time limit on such intimacy and endearment;
how does it all slip away?
What a true disaster it is when you become the monster you
feared you would, and everything slips through your fingers.
What a tragedy that one sentence can end an entire lifetime of
happiness.
What a calamity, that you feel like you'll never be the same.
But, darling, you will not be, you will be better.
How empowering is it that you are alive.

Love of

The love of your confidence.
The love of your laughter.
The love of our fireworks.
The love of all our moments
and our love that'll never leave my mind.
The simplicity within a profound love.
What a true honour
to have experienced this great a love,
and be able to grow from its accompanying heartbreak.

Align

Planets align
Gravity seems suddenly nonexistent
It is not the planets
That are pulling each other
Or the effect of the sun or the moon,
Just utter compliance.
Order.
The simple way
Things are supposed to be.
You and me
For a moment it felt like a supernova
Like the planets aligned
Just for us.

K. Ross

Absent

Disposable.
As if one could hand me off to another
Trivial.
As I waited for you,
Dazed.
I always wondered what it'd be like to have a bad habit;
A habit so addicting that you'd give up your life for it
Your body would yearn for it
Your mind would be always on it
A power so strong you'd give up anything-
Everything.
Give up something that you held in your arms,
Something to which you gave life.
Why'd you give me up?

Have you ever consumed the things that consume you?

Do we ever fully understand or anticipate the repercussions of our actions?

Good kid

I think I was such a "good" kid because
I saw what I wanted.
An outsider
Who saw a mommy that would lay down herw own life to
nurture,
And provide
To give everything she had for her child.
Through my youthful eyes
I witnessed children who didn't know the value
What they were given
Despite all their complaining, screaming, and crying
After all their antics,
No matter what the trouble
They were always forgiven.
They could do no wrong,
But I could.
MI've been in many houses
Belonging to many friends.
All of their mothers
praised the "good" child I was
But I could never be
And I never was
Their child,
The one they truly loved.

K. Ross

Reflection in What Matters

A mother; beautiful, angelic, free.
Women are wildly caring and kind.
Always hearing her child's plea.
A human who never leaves—we cannot rewind.

A clear window that could have been,
Lifetime of looking in at others,
Photographs of laughter and love, in a scene,
Cruelty in the form of society, smothers.

Yet I had you, the opposite of a mother
Nonetheless so nurturing and supportive,
Someone who never led me astray.
With the warmth you were carrying,
If love was currency, everyday would be payday.

Bearing a child doesn't make you a mother
But unlike a babe, I can't have another.

Chances

Chances
When does one run out?
Where is the line?
How is it defined?
One or two or three ?

Are chances defined by numbers?
Or the depth of situations?
Are chances given in baker's dozen?
One more just in case

Are chances given
In the hope of change
And improvement for the future?

Chances are hope's sister
The idea that
With time
Things will be better
That one has learned from
Their wrongs

Chances
Blindly allow
Someone to change their original
Choice
To believe that
If given the same situation
They will do right by you
Because chances my darling
Are just your heart
Pulling
And grasping
It's your heart pleading
To not let go.

10/09

October ninth—
A normal day to others
But I –
I must
Breathe deeply
It is a day
That I
Must remember
The two
Unfinished loves of my life

Shards

You broke my heart
Multiple times
Each time
I collected the shards
Of my hope and dreams for us
Until you took your last breath.
It was almost like it was mine,
Your final strives
To tear my heart strings one last time

I have grieved enough for a lifetime

Azizam

I loved you harder
than I had loved anybody in a very long time.
It was quick, it was steady.
I saw things in you that I admired.
Who I wanted to be.
Be like you.
You were someone who could simply walk into a room and
everyone would gasp for air.
You were intoxicating.

I had never met anyone like you.
There had been other people in my past considered
beautiful, popular, humble, even all three,
but you were and still are extraordinary.
No one ever measured up, and I still have not encountered
someone as persevering, honest, and heartfelt as you.

For a long time,
I had been searching for a friend that I could be my genuine
self with, someone I did not have to worry about giving too
much to.
From the moment I met you,
I knew that I wouldn't need to worry.
It was like my home was within you.

Love language

Silly boys,
They thought her love language was gifts
And then labelled it as something else.
Yes, gifts were nice
It was a type of love she knew
It was something real
Something she was able to hold on to
But if you really knew her
You'd know
It was deeper
Her love language was
Consistency
Stability
Allowance of flexibility
And acts of love
That you had to show
And prove
Everyday
Because if you didn't,
It reminded her of the love she lacked
The fear of everything around crumbling
And how quickly
Her stability
Could come crashing
Down.

Broken mirrors

My loves goes out to
all the little girls
that searched for a mirror image
of who they were,
but may have had it warped
by their insecurities
and lack of self-worth.

K. Ross

Eyes

The love I had for you was friendly
A deep endearing kind
But little did I know
You were wrapped up
In a kind disguise.
You were undressing me with your eyes.

Route

I always used to feel like
Being lost was a bad thing
Lacking a sense of direction
Or not knowing where you are headed
This was
Until I met you.
Taking a wrong turn
Going in circles
Or not being sure of where.
What way we were taking
When we were together
Was not a fuss.
Because with you,
It never feels like I'm lost,
But just taking a longer route.

K. Ross

Abyss

People trust that allowing for space strengthens relationships,
but what happens when that space becomes a universe,
and you cannot navigate your way back?
Is the solar system a circle which falls back into its original
placement?
Or, for that moment in time we were everything,
and now it's over.
Too far gone,
Darkness surrounds me
And I find myself,
Forever stuck in this abyss.

Falsehood

Saying 'I love you'
Out of obligation
Out of fear of rejection
Out of fear of losing someone
Out of anything
Anything without pure
Intention and devotion
Is a lie.
That will brand your future
With all the falsehoods
Of your past.

K. Ross

Broken

I never really had a good reason to not feel worthy of love.
A fear deeply internalized.
Love was something you saw
on television screens of beautiful girls,
and the boys who couldn't live without them.

Love was Christmastime
with your mom and dad and siblings
wrapped around the tall tree surrounded by presents.

Love was having a dozen friends
who fought over you during gym class.

Love was a concept to me that I did not fit into.

Early in life it's hard to narrow down love.
Being young and gullible,
trying to pinpoint what draws people in,
Constantly questioning
what is it that brings people to cherish you,
And most of all
what makes someone loveable.

Sea Shore

I'm the type of person
Who holds your clothes
While you jump into the sea
Searching for love

I watched you jump
Into the sea for love
Hoping that one day
You'd return to shore
And see
That everything you could
Ever want
Was me.
Here I was waiting on land.

How stupid you were to look anywhere else.

Deep Amber

Waiting for the person
Who sees my eyes as pools of honey
The organic kind,
Bittersweet
Just like me

Don't act colorblind, never let red flags leave you in a grey area.

Idolization

Idolization—
The death of a person's real self.
An image of the perfection I once saw you as,
And you envisioned of me
An ideal that we could not uphold
Which caused our downfall
It was no longer
You and I
Above all.

Dreamt

Naïve was I;
A decade of a difference
And I thought you could take care of me
The way I yearned for
But the beauty I saw in you
Wasn't your reflection
It wasn't all the things that composed you
It was the attributes I gave you
I excused your avoidance
For a fear of love
I allowed the silence
Made it bonding
I painted the way you put me last
As your dedication for work
I didn't laugh
But I thought not all likeliness is the same
I was patient
I was kind
I was beautiful
I was what I thought you wanted
Yet I missed that
You cannot try to be an ideal
And you cannot make someone that way
The way I sculpted you in my mind
Was never who you were
But it was I
And who I dreamed to love

K. Ross

Wildfire

I wanted to be so consumed by love
Deeply embedded in the other person
As if day and night were one
And we were a solar eclipse
Discover a love that is deep
And sincere,
So cohesive that time gets lost

You were a wildfire
Mid-spring
Warm yet destructive
Hypnotizing
The way you would
Engulf everything around you

Obsession of wanting to please you
Wanting every
Single
Moment
To be graced with you
And I
To be so lucky
To be
In your atmosphere
And inhale your smoke

Bliss

Dimly lit room
Sunset that glares through
Your tiny window
Gentle breeze
Warmth flooding the room
Gentle caress
Your ocean blue eyes watch me
As I drift away
Tiptoe
Giggles as you pull me
Back to you
The waves of your white sheets
Smell of lavender
The day is done
Your raspy gentle whisper
Making it feel like
There are endless possibilities
The day has just begun

Who knew that the butterflies in my stomach would cause my heart to explode

Burning in my throat

You were intoxicating
Like a teenage girl taking her first tequila shot
The anticipation as
The fiery sensation is dripping down her throat
The heat
The warm energy
The excitement of something with a danger warning
Something I felt like I could touch
But not hold on to
A bottle with a flame
Fire on a matchstick
Yet surrounded by naivete
I was surprised when I was burned by your flame

K. Ross

Knotted

And just like that,
It seemed we were knots.
Intertwined.
You were everywhere
Everything
Even beneath my surface
The excitement of you
As if you were my Purkinje fibers
The pressure of you
Keeping me alive
Pure electricity
The essence of my very being
Yet,
When time passed,
you were exposed as something entirely different.
The pressure I felt was risk.
Hazard.
You were the cortisol in my body,
Slight highs
Major lows
And lessons for a lifetime

Unwavering

I constantly made my lovers into best friends,
Yet was surprised when their love faded,
And they vanished,
While my love remained.

Craving

The worst
Is craving
A love so deep
Sincere
Gentle
Yet all-consuming
As though one moment
You are drenched in sunlight
Warmed by the
Radiation
Then all of a sudden
There is an
Absence of light
Engulfed by the
Brightness of the moon
Radiating
In the darkest times
There is still
Luminance

Fear

I have a fear of being:
Fear of being too clingy
Too attached
Too much of an overachiever
Too outgoing
Too nice
Too accommodating
Too trusting
Too tall
Too skinny
Being too much
Too much.
A fear of being.

Fear cont.

Fear.
A word defined as an unpleasant, often strong, emotion caused
by Anticipation or awareness of danger
The human mind creates its own dangers;
I had become Someone I did not recognize
And you, my dear, recognized me,
But it was not as someone you loved,
Yet as someone you'd grown to tolerate.
Indiscretion and desire for something more than small talk
And arguments
You couldn't fix me
I simply needed to grow
Alone.
I possessed a type of fear
The kind that swallows you whole
And by the time you realize
You're head deep
In a sinkhole
The more you panic
The deeper you sink

Deep breaths now,
And try not to think.

It scares me, the lack of drive I seem to have.
It scares me that one day I'll either have everything or nothing.

Rip out my heart
and see the scar tissue left behind by my existence
As if I do not breathe oxygen, but instead glass.

The Water Fountain is Empty

Waiting for the days I will not need to sleep the hours away

K. Ross

Numbing

I don't remember why,
but after a while I couldn't feel anything.
I don't think anyone noticed
I became numb to my surroundings.
I didn't know why I was doing things.
Did I not think I was good enough?

This kind of utter darkness, eating me from the inside out.
Constantly floating along.
I remember I had told you I felt numb,
but I don't think you understood the lack of motivation
or the emptiness I had dug myself into.

As if I were drifting in space— roaming up,
down, left, or right—just me.
Stuck wondering
which way will set me free.
I have to say,
I was always someone who felt like I was drowning in one way
or another.
Silently bobbing
as the only things not underwater
were my nose and mouth.

I had developed a sort of constant hatred for myself.
It was me trying to steady my breath just right,
keeping myself alive.

V Mentality

Don't play the victim.
It's hard.
For a very long time I felt as if the world was against me.
As if someone owed me something
because there were things that others had that I didn't.
And I didn't turn this into anger, but instead self-hatred,
self-judgement, and the ongoing odds that I didn't deserve the future.
Every time I attempted something, I immediately assumed that I couldn't do it.
I was always in a state of you don't know what it's like to be me.
As if I was the only one struggling with who I was, and where I was going.
That horrible endless cycle of being negative and being my own worst enemy.
It had to stop.
No, you cannot change where you come from and the events that make you who you are,
but you can know where you're going and put all your energy into shaping your future.
It gets better.
But you have to believe in what can be, instead of being stuck in what was.

Misconstruction

Do not be hurt
By people underestimating your struggle
By others not being able
To grasp
The intricate moments
That have built your life
Do not be hurt
By others speaking about their own
Struggles and assuming
Yours could never measure up
Do not be hurt
About a misconstruction
Of who you are
From people
Who do not look to understand,
But to assume
Others who maintain in their bubble
As it would not serve
Them otherwise
Do not be hurt
Embrace others
Appreciate instead the struggle of others
And know
Although they have their own endeavors,
Have not hurt like you
Because to know that hurt
Is like a sharp dagger
Forever pierced in your heart
Do not be hurt my love,
As they will always
Label it as jewelry

Load to bear

I felt alone for most of my life
Almost as if I had a load, I couldn't put on anyone else to bear
But I was mistaken in a sense
I always had a solid foundation
I never felt like I was sinking, and I had to pry myself
Except for in the devastating walls of my mind

Lifetimes

I have lived a thousand lifetimes
All my secrets linger in the wind
Mini clips
Of scenes I have seen
Emotions I have felt
But when I
Attempt to describe
The thousands
Of lifetimes—
Silence
Nothing slips through my lips
Just my heart
Filled with despair

Beauties

For all my beautiful friends,
The ones who are so much more
Than the beauty they possess on the outside,
For every time a man professed love
That was solely based on your outer parts
For every time a man wanted to access your body
And not your soul
For every girl who didn't think
She was beautiful based on a man's assessment of her
The ones who are
So much more than
The beauty they possess on the outside
But the beauty embedded deep inside them

Questioning

Pins and needles
Inside my chest
Constant unrest
When will I ever be
The person I desire to be?
When will I
Glance
Into any
Reflective surface
And not be
Surprised by the person I see?
Low-hanging eyes
Left in the past,
When will I ever be
    Proud of me?

The Water Fountain is Empty

I love you

I was lost and alone
With nowhere to go
But when I looked into your eyes
I truly knew there was a god
And I was whole

Now it's me and you
And I wouldn't have it any other way
Because I know the truth
And I see it everyday

You are my world and I am yours
I will always be with you
And of this you can be sure
What we share is too much

I remember everything in my life
But when God gave me you
I began to live within your light

I love you so much
You will never know
You gave me strength when I was low
I can't believe it
I didn't know
How someone so precious could fill my soul.

-W.A.R

You and me against the world

Transience

I constantly think about
How each year slips away
How the seconds turn into minutes and eventually
That is our whole lives
and how the amount of time
we get to spend together
Gets smaller
Silently disappearing
The large amount we
Assumed we had is no longer present
It is the human condition
To feel mortality
To have an out of body experience
When truly considering
How much time is left
And how we have previously spent the precious
seconds that turned into minutes and eventually
That is our whole lives

But the memories never fade

We never think we can survive something, until we do.

Uncertainty

When I was younger
I used to have dreams about
Going places,
But I'd never have shoes on
It was like I wasn't
Prepared
For where I was going,
Or where I was coming from.

K. Ross

Treading

I feel like I am treading
I cannot tell
If this pool
Is shallow as a pond
Or as deep
As the ocean,
Yet I know
With one false step
I will sink under
Mini bubbles rising
Never touching the surface

Vinegar

I'll always remember your laugh,
The way you ate your French fries with too much vinegar,
How you taught me to eat toast with butter and sugar.
You taught me how to rollerblade
And took me everywhere with them
When I wouldn't take them off.
In the times you tried to be there,
In the times you put together the strength
And resilience to give me moments I will cherish,
To giving me the strength to not need anyone,
But also the courage to believe in myself.
You gave me life, even though you couldn't give me guidance.
Our choices define our lives, and the lives of our children.
Even though your choices ended your life,
In a way they gave me the chance to live mine,
Extraordinary and unapologetically,
Sour like the vinegar you loved,
And sweet like the sugar on toast you taught me to love.

K. Ross

Waiting

You always knew where to find me,
Although I didn't always know where you were
I found myself,
In the middle of my ordinary day,
Looking out the window,
Sitting on the ledge
Waiting for you.
Time shifting forward.
Shadows of life
Swiftly passing
Minutes turned into hours
Sometimes days
Stuck sitting
Waiting
But I knew when the time came
You would find me
And time,
Those minutes that turned into hours
And sometimes into days,
Would fade

A penny in the water fountain

Just six years old.
Pennies stick to the bottom of the fountain
"Go ahead,
Throw a penny in for a wish,"
She says
I close my eyes
The brass penny makes the water ripple
I hear the
The light sound as
The water trickles
Slowly the penny drifts to the bottom
I stare into our rippled reflection
Closing my eyes,
I think to myself,
I wish life was always like this

K. Ross

Windmill

I may have been five,
The day you took me away.
It was raining
I remember your concern,
The ideas that you made up in your head about him
Was he abusing me?
I remember trusting you blindly,
Going wherever you took me,
Until you left.
I think this is my first memory.
A month before I could return to him,
And I remember,
The windmill turning in the wind.
Blue, Green, Pink, Yellow
A young girl ripped from her home,
Yet, it was so soft and so delicate,
Only someone you love and trusted
Could do such damage
So seductively.

Funny thing about things coming to an end is
You were never aware of it,
You just sit back and brace for impact, and when it's over
Reminisce on the days you'll never get back.

K. Ross

When you're strong no one asks you how you're doing.

Glow

I learned from an early age
Quietly observing
Watching
One simple thing
Beauty comes from within
A glow
A shine
A radiating confidence
A comfort in who you are
Like hydrogen atoms reacting within the sun to produce light

Trophy

Burn hair
Burn calories
Just so someone would burn for you

I always craved for
Someone to reach into my heart
And caress my soul

Pretty face
Pretty laugh
On the outside to others

A canvas to paint
Clay to mould
A trophy to polish

No one to ever reach my soul
But to simply
To take pride
In my outer layers
That one day would be no more
How incredibly ignorant
To not look
For more

Repression

Repression,
My best friend,
You have saved me
From my darkest thoughts,
And kept me strong
In my weakest moments
Repression,
Buried deep
Tiny memories
That could break me
Repression,
You have saved me

My future is so bright that
no one *dares* ask about the shadows of my past

Assumptions

A lot of people assume that I was a good kid, and I was
But there were certain things I could've fallen into.
I watch people around me and I could've been just like them
One choice
One way
One different action could have changed everything about me.
My awareness for what I've been through,
And the dangers of my inner sorrow saved me,
My urge for control and consistency,
The way I craved things to
Be the same and not have anything interrupt.
I knew what destruction I could do to myself.
Slit my wrists,
Take drugs—self-medicate to numb,
Sleep with boys that said they loved me,
Find temporary things,
Things that would make me okay for a moment.
Instead, I sat in my misery
I endured my panic attacks
And painted my despair with laughter.
Only those who were close to me ever knew,
And I don't even think they really knew.
Every day I made a choice.
For a more lethal detriment
Between an inner or external destruction.

Slip

I always fell in love with the idea of potential
The possibility of growth
Someone's ideal self
I could always see what could be
Which meant a lot of the time
It clouded what actually was
Fixing people
Waiting for better
Seeing the best
And always waiting for more
That's why people are so disappointing
They are not what you see in them
Or make them up to be
They are the actions they take
And the habits they keep
You cannot love someone into being better
Even if it benefits them
All the encouragement,
Love, and sacrifice will not mould them into the ideal you see.
You can only wait,
Give them the support they may need,
See how far they will let themselves grow,
And pray you're around to see it.

Insufficient funds
I am a bank card that is no longer able to give.
You may not withdraw what you need,
And not deposit anything in return.

Seeking

I never felt
What other girls did.
I never felt an intense
Want,
A need to interact with someone
Based on their looks
I have never found
Attraction from a glimpse
I have seen beautiful strangers,
I have been in awe of the features
They possess,
Yet that has never been
Enough.
I was never boy crazy
Or liked someone
Due to their features
Am I missing something?

I was almost the opposite.
It was like I would lose interest
Quicker.
I always admired people's
Characters
I'm not certain if it was
My love language
Or subconscious—
I just could not latch on
To an ideal.
I craved something real
I always wondered if there was
Something different about me.
Why couldn't I experience what they did?
Why couldn't I have what they show in movies?

The Water Fountain is Empty

I crave depth,
Sincerity,
Fearlessness,
Stability,
And most of all,
A sense of self—
Something simple that
A handsome face could never
Reveal to me.

K. Ross

The one I love

Why is it
That when I name
Things and people
I love
The list never includes myself?
I can forgive
And forget
The mistakes of others
Conceal them
As if they
Deserve more kindness
And compassion than I

Why is it
That I cannot
Forgive myself for simple
Things,
Like forgetting,
Making mistakes?
What will it take?
What does it mean to finally be
The one I love,
The one I adore,
The person who deserves
Forgiveness,
Love,
Devotion,
And most of all,
The person who deserves
What she craves?
Understanding

Forms

I struggled
I struggled all my life to find a place
That I fit into
I struggled all my life
To pinpoint what love was
To pinpoint family
To navigate my own being
I have found that
Love is in many forms
It is food,
It is shelter,
It is someone slightly yelling to get your act together,
It is holding doors,
It is checking in,
It is allowing someone to vent,
It is gentle glances across the room to see if the other is okay
Love is little moments—
Those tiny moments,
They add up
To love

Whispers

I tried to calmly whisper
Instead, it came out as
Silence
Deepening breaths
As I hesitated to express
What has
And will always
Linger in the back
Of my mind
A muffled fear
But you didn't hear
You loudened your cry
Over mine
Too quickly
Abrupt
You interrupted
And made me realize:
How can I
Express who am I
When others
Don't open their mind?

Devotion is daunting

I am worried.
I am worried about
Future lovers
And their tendencies to sprint for one hundred meters
To forget that this is a marathon.
I am scared that people get comfortable
Forgetting how to love.
I am scared people see their partner's situation
But do not seek to understand
Bottling this into a complaint
Their hands are tied
And accusing me of not knowing how to love.
I am terrified that I will walk this earth for the rest of my life
To never find a human being that
Respects and honors me, like I do them.
I am terrified that the magic of devotion and care
Has faded in this generation.
And I am ultimately afraid to give a piece of myself
To someone
Or anyone who dares put it on a shelf.
My love
My sanity
Are wrapped around each other
Questioning how
I will ever
Keep them both
Intact

Family.
A word that everyone seems to be able to define,
but is different in concept for many.

To my wings

To lose a parent
Is to lose a limb,
Yet by your grace
I have been given
Wings
I have yet to fall,
You have guided and nourished me
Through it all
You are the reason
For my strive
And for that
I owe you my
Life
I am eternally indebted
For you have been a type
of heaven
The safe place
That everyone prays for
And not all get to experience,
With love and kindness and laughter
A home that is not made up of four walls
But within our very being,
A love that is heavy
And tenderness that is all-consuming
I promise to always take
Care of you
Because, after all,
Who am I
Without you?

Wither

There is tragedy in dying young
Suddenly
Before your time
Maybe without warning
Many years ahead of you not yet lived.

But the true heart-wrenching way
To have someone
Exit this life
Is slowly—
Watching them slowly wither
Being betrayed by their own mind
Their own body
Falling apart

Many years of what made
Them alive
Memories
Thoughts
Emotions
All the people they had met
All becomes nothing

The cruel truth of life
Is that death
Quickly follows

T'es capables

I whispered to myself,
"Hold your head up high, this is the best part."

The present

I have to say, I spent so much time being the person that was defined by my past. I was someone who was their circumstances. A poor girl, a Black girl, a skinny girl. I always allowed my past to predict how I would act and how I saw myself. In some cases, this was fine, I could get through the day. But these schemas I had of myself may have been the death of me. No matter how well I did, or the obvious potential I had, I never could believe in myself to do better. I was stuck, like this type of quicksand. The more I moved, the more I would overthink and sink.

Sinking, deeper and deeper, until one day while my head was sticking out of the sand- I decided it was enough.

Enough thinking about how hard my life is, and how I do not have a chance. I took the things that were in the present and the hope of the future and tried to move forward. Strived towards a better day.

One thing I learned is that you cannot live in fear of one day failing, and ruin everyday you have now.

Whole

There are some people you meet in life that make you feel whole. When you are together it is like your whole past makes sense and every struggle that you went through was to get to them.

The beauty they bring to your life cannot be measured or weighed.

It's a love that is unspeakable and delightful.

Restoration

I sensed
My whole world was caving in,
But just as the sun sets,
It will rise again.
The horizon
Bright
With oranges and reds,
The burning fire
Of what tomorrow has to bring.
A reminder that with every ending,
There is a hope for a brand new day.

K. Ross

Although I may no longer feel the same as when I wrote these poems, I'm so glad I can look back and see my journey. Being able to reflect is one of the beauties of life. My one hope for everyone is that they can reflect and grow from their past, no matter the circumstances.

www.ingramcontent.com/pod-product-compliance
Lightning Source LLC
Chambersburg PA
CBHW071533120626
46550CB00006B/2444